Jesus Loves the Nephites

written by Tiffany Thomas
illustrated by Nikki Casassa

CFI · An imprint of Cedar Fort, Inc. · Springville, Utah

HARD WORDS:
blessing, disciple, sacrament

PARENT TIP: Point out that two, too, and to are three different words that sound the same, but each different meaning has a different spelling.

Jesus comes to the Nephites.

They feel His hands and feet.

Jesus teaches the people.

He tells the sick people
to come to Him.

He heals the sick people.

He also gives a blessing to every child.

He teaches the
people how to pray.

Jesus calls
twelve good men
to be disciples.

He gives them the sacrament.

Jesus goes back to live with God.

The people are very good
for a long time.

The end.

ISBN 13: 978-1-4621-4337-5

Published by CFI, an imprint of Cedar Fort, Inc. • 2373 W. 700 S., Suite 100, Springville, UT 84663
Distributed by Cedar Fort, Inc., www.cedarfort.com

Cover design and interior layout design by Shawnda T. Craig
Cover design © 2022 Cedar Fort, Inc.
Printed in China • Printed on acid-free paper
10 9 8 7 6 5 4 3 2 1